Podcast Domination

By
Marc Guberti

Your Free Gift

As a way of thanking you for your purchase, I am offering you a free ticket to the Content Marketing Success Summit.

The Content Marketing Success Summit showcases an ever growing list of speakers who will teach you how to create, promote, and optimize your content—and use that content to generate a full-time income.

If you are interested in achieving a full-time income from your content brand, then I recommend getting your free ticket for the **Content Marketing Success Summit** which contains the insights that will allow you to reach the next level.

contentmarketingsuccesssummit.com

Table Of Contents

Introduction

Podcasting presents wonderful opportunities and allows you to build relationships with influencers in your niche. John Lee Dumas, Pat Flynn, and others demonstrated that podcasting could also bring in a full-time income. That's what I knew, and that's what people kept telling me.

I made three attempts at starting a podcast. For the first podcast idea, the show structure was that I interview people. For the second podcast idea, I would answer my listeners' questions and do a daily episode. None of those ideas ever got implemented. The first podcast idea looked like a pipe dream. While I did some of the episodes for the second podcast idea, it never materialized, and I didn't know how to publish podcast episodes anyway.

Enter Podcast Idea #3. I swung and missed twice, but I didn't strike out. Podcast Idea #3 was none other than Breakthrough Success. I've had the privilege of interviewing hundreds of influencers in my niche and some of my role models. The podcast has changed my life, and I know starting a podcast can dramatically change your life as well.

When I started my podcast, I was 18 years old. I had written thousands of blog posts and over a dozen books before that point. I already had a booming content brand but felt like something was missing. Thus, Breakthrough Success was born, and I haven't looked back.

As I fell more in love with podcasting, I turned Breakthrough Success from a weekly show to a weekday show. That meant going from just publishing one episode per week to publishing five episodes per week. It was a big shift that was possible because of the two virtual summits I hosted just before making that jump. I got more conformable with interviewing more than five people every week and knew this would be great for the Breakthrough Success Podcast.

For most of my content brand's existence, I focused on blogging, video, social media, and other things as well. Now I also teach people how to grow their brands with a podcast. That's the focus of this book and probably why you're reading it. You want to launch, grow, and monetize your podcast. You want to learn that same lesson so your podcast grows your brand or even becomes your brand.

I've said a few things about myself and my podcasting journey. Now let's begin shaping yours.

Chapter 1
Setting It Up And Preparing For Each Episode

Before we discuss how to use podcasting to grow your brand, we first need to talk about the set up. What will your podcast be about? How will you publish the episodes? There are several questions you need to address before we can discuss landing guests and promoting each episode.

Determining Your Podcast's Topic
Some people already know the answers to these questions while others need to dig a little deeper. The topic you choose for your podcast is important because you're committed to it for a while. Breakthrough Success focuses on how entrepreneurs achieved their success while revealing some of these people's backstories in the process.

You may choose a completely different topic, but you need to decide and commit. You'll either be committed to this topic for many years, or, much worse, you'll realize you picked the wrong topic after publishing dozens of episodes. Then you either dispassionately continue or you scrap all of your work.

That's not the type of decision you want to make.

That's why I advise you take great care in determining your podcast's topic. Is this something you'd be happy to talk about and listen about for many years? If so, that's your topic. You'll discover that topic for you by writing down all of the potential podcast topics you can cover. Once you pick the topic, write down potential names for your podcast until you find one that strikes you.

Write as many topic ideas as possible. Even if you are already committed to one topic, you may find a better topic or expand on your original concept.

Finding A Great Podcast Hosting Site
Once you determine your podcast's topic, the next step is to find a reliable podcast hosting site. While there are many options available, I recommend Libsyn. With Libsyn, you can get your podcast hosted for as little as $5 each month.

You can even use Libsyn to get your podcast on places like iTunes, Spotify, Stitcher, and more. This is a staple feature for many podcast hosting options, but it's best to do some digging first. Pippa, Podbean, PodOmatic, Buzzsprout, and Blubrry are some of the other podcast hosting options available.

Even though most podcast hosting sites do a fine job with providing tutorial videos for getting your podcast on iTunes, Spotify, Stitcher, and others, there's one place your podcast must be on. That one place is TuneIn. Why TuneIn? That's the one Amazon's Echo smart speaker uses to play podcasts. If you say, "Alexa play the podcast Breakthrough Success," Alexa is pulling the podcast from TuneIn. iHeart Radio is also a great place to put your podcast to leverage smart speakers.

One important thing to note is that with any of these podcast hosting sites, you'll still have to head over to GoDaddy if you want to own the domain name of your podcast. You can either buy a new domain name that matches up with your podcast or offer a Podcast tab on your existing website. I've found the latter to be more effective since it keeps people on my blog where they can consume additional content.

Quality Audio Matters

You don't need the best audio in the world which some people spend thousands of dollars to achieve, but you can't have poor audio. Poor audio will turn listeners away from your podcast, no matter how great the actual content is.

Great audio has become the expectation, and the best way to fulfill that expectation is with the Blue Yeti Microphone. Yes, there are better microphones, but this microphone gives you incredible sound quality for about $100. Most of the other top quality microphones cost several hundreds dollars which isn't the type of budget you want for just starting a podcast.

If you have guests on your show, make sure they also have quality audio on their end. For these types of shows, understand that the guest will do most of the talking. The guest's audio will reflect the quality of your show. If the guest's audio is great, people won't crowd your social media feed with "Great audio" comments, but they will stick around. If the guest's audio is bad, your listeners won't stick around.

Recording Episodes

When you do a solo podcast, you have plenty of options for recording interviews. You can use QuickTime, iMovie, Movie Maker, Screenflow, Camtasia, your smartphone, and a bunch of other options. When you don't interview someone, all you do is find your favorite way to record and start talking.

If you have a guest on your episodes, it's different. I didn't know what that difference was when I first wanted to launch a podcast. Not knowing that difference and not having enough desire to do the research prevented me from starting my own podcast in the beginning. That won't be you, because I'll provide you with all you need to know about interviewing people if that's the direction you want to take.

There are two recording options available. The first option is Skype's Call Recorder which is the cheaper of the two options at $39.95. Skype's Call Recorder allows you to record conversations, and you can set it up to automatically record conversations so you don't have to remember. This solution works for most podcast hosts. The only issue with Skype is that video interviews can get laggy and there will be some moments (a few seconds) where you can't hear what the guest is saying.

People have reported other problems with Skype such as calls randomly dropping, but in my experience of interviewing over 200 guests on Skype, I've never had a call get randomly dropped.

Zoom is the other option which comes at a $14.99/mo price point. Zoom is much better if you plan on conducting video interviews so you can see the guest on the other side. If your episodes are less than 40 minutes in length, you can use the free version, but know that the free version automatically drops conversations within 40 minutes. That's Zoom's way of saying you should buy the paid version.

Zoom doesn't give me many problems and is my go-to for recording video interviews which were frequent during my two virtual summits. While Skype requires that you connect with the other person, Zoom requires that you send a link to the guest, and they'll join the call by clicking on the link. These are subtle differences that you should know about when making your decision, although this particular difference shouldn't have much of a say in the final decision. It should come down to do you want to interview people audio only or do you want to conduct video interviews. That's where the differences between these two options becomes more significant.

Chapter 2

Getting Guests On Your Show

While it is possible to launch a solo podcast, it is better to have guests on your show. Inviting guests to come on your podcast allows you to build relationships and provide your listeners with more value. The more people you interview, the more you learn.

The initial challenge you'll face if you want guests on your podcast is getting guests on your show. Getting guests on your show comes down to finding the right people and crafting the right ask. For this chapter, we'll start with some of the ways you can find guests for your show and then discuss how to craft the right ask.

Find Other Podcasts
One of the most surefire ways to find guests for your podcast is to see who's been on other podcasts. I look at a few business podcasts and reach out to those guests. There are plenty of ways to find other podcasts, but these are the best ways to find podcasts and save time too.

#1: iTunes: The largest podcast directory that keeps on growing. Many podcasters uses this platform to attract more listeners to their shows. You can leverage iTunes' rich range of content by finding podcasts in your niche.

#2: Stitcher, Spotify, and others: While iTunes is the top place for podcasting, not everyone has an Apple device. If you only put your podcast on iTunes, you lose everyone who uses Microsoft, Android, and other devices that aren't Apple devices. Many of the top podcasts on iTunes also find their way on Stitcher, Spotify, and plenty of others. Ever since Spotify made it easier for any podcaster to get their show on the app, Spotify has become a great opportunity for podcasters.

#3: Google: Because you can use Google to find just about anything. The difference Google provides is that you might come across articles listing the Top 10 Podcasts in your niche. Not only are these lists valuable for finding great podcasts in your niche, but also reach out to the people who created those lists. Your success is based on the relationships you build.

#4: LinkedIn: The most underutilized social network on the web for relationship building. LinkedIn is a search engine that shows people based on the search results. Searching a phrase like business podcast host will show you a list of business podcast hosts. LinkedIn is also a great place to become a guest on many podcasts which we'll talk about later.

Virtual Summits
Once you've looked through several podcasts in your niche, the next step is to look for virtual summits in your niche. While in-person events and conferences can be great places to find potential guests, virtual summits are the best place to find great guests.

Most virtual summit sessions are conducted as interviews. That means each speaker at a virtual summit has been interviewed in a similar style to a podcast interview. You can find speakers at in-person events and conferences who have been interviewed. However, it's possible you run into someone who does a lot of public speaking but doesn't do interviews.

Guest Blogs

You'll find more guests than you could ever interview by sticking with everything else. If you want to add some flare and interview guests who everyone else hasn't interviewed yet, you can find guest blogs in your niche and contact some of the contributors.

My only warning with this approach is that some of the contributors may have never been interviewed before and don't have the right audio set-up. However, you can find some top talent with this approach and be one of the few podcasts to have had that person as a guest. Additionally, since these people don't get as many interview requests, they tend to say yes more often unless they don't like doing interviews.

Facebook Groups

While many people exclusively think about Facebook ads when viewing the social network as a business asset, Facebook Groups are commonly overlooked. We will talk more later about starting your own Facebook Group to build a stronger community around your podcast, but for now, we'll talk about using Facebook Groups to land more guests on your podcast.

Start by finding active and targeted Facebook Groups. Once you find at least 10 groups, commit to the Daily 3-3-3 Plan. Every day, you go into various Facebook Groups to create three posts, leave three comments on other people's posts, and react to three other posts by liking, loving, wowing, etc.

As you follow the Daily 3-3-3 Plan overtime, you'll become a well-known member in several Facebook Groups. Some people in the group will reach out to you through Messenger to build the relationship further. These people can make great guests for your podcast.

You can also reach out to some people in the group and invite them to be guests on your podcast. When following the Daily 3-3-3 Plan, be intentional with the posts you are commenting and reacting to. People will notice if you comment or react to their posts, so if you want a particular person as a guest on your podcast, engaging with their posts in the group is a great way to start the relationship.

As you master the Daily 3-3-3 Plan, you may bump it up to a Daily 4-4-4 Plan or even a Daily 5-5-5 Plan. However, maintain 3-3-3 as a bare minimum. If you reach 4-4-4 or 5-5-5, do it for a few days, but can then only do 3-3-3 on one day, don't beat yourself up. 3-3-3 is the bare minimum, and you might do more than that on some days. Don't compensate by giving yourself double the work the following day. The reason I don't want you to compensate is if you miss three days, you'll feel like you need to pull off a 12-12-12 which doesn't make it as consistent or fun.

As you join and engage in more Facebook Groups, pay attention to how they are run. Pay attention to how members engage with one another and the group rules. Pay attention to how being a part of that Facebook Group makes you feel. What do you like and not like about the group? How do the group admins promote their products if at all? Paying attention to subtleties like these will help when you decide to create a Facebook Group for your podcast listeners.

Ask For Referrals

Once you incorporate some or all of the above tactics to find guests for your show and make the right ask (more on that coming up), you'll have the pre and post interview conversations. Most people use the pre-interview conversation to highlight how the episode will flow. However, you can use the post-interview conversation to ask guests if they know anyone who would be a great fit for your show. Most guests will be happy to recommend a few good fits.

Making The Ask

Before you can ask your guests for referrals, you first need to ask people to be guests on your podcast. While getting the yes gets easier as you interview more people, many people are happy to be on a podcast of any size...even if your podcast is in the pre-launch stage.

Before asking anyone, start by asking the people in your network. I built relationships in advance, and some of those people were among the first guests on my show. As I tapped into existing relationships, I also reached out to people I didn't know before and asked them to be on my podcast.

The way you craft your ask depends in part on how long your podcast has been around. If your podcast is new, mention that it is going to get launched soon and the potential guest would be among the first episodes. It also helps if you've followed the potential guest for a while and wanted to know if they are interested in being on your podcast. Here's how I asked people to be on Breakthrough Success in the early days:

> Hello [name],
>
> I am starting a podcast and am interviewing various experts who want to talk about how they achieved their breakthrough while providing advice. I have been following you for a while [personalize the email explaining how you've been following them. Finish the sentence and add one more if you desire. The shorter, the better]. I would love to have you as a guest if your schedule allows.
>
> Warm regards,
> Marc Guberti

If your podcast is more established, tell potential guests who some of the previous guests on the show were. When you mention past guests on your podcast, potential guests see an opportunity to boost their authority due to the association factor. If people are interviewed on the same podcast as the leaders in your niche, they get a boost in their authority. You can see authority by association in full effect when you go on a website and see the "As featured in" tab which shows podcast and media logos.

You should also demonstrate your credibility as you make the ask. I didn't do this in my previous ask, but I made the change as I made more requests. Here is the ask I currently leverage:

> I am a X-year-old entrepreneur with over 500K social media followers and over 10K subscribers. If you are interested, I would be honored to have you as a guest on the Breakthrough Success Podcast.
>
> Past guests on the show include [past guests on Breakthrough Success the potential guest may know, and many others. Please let me know if you are interested and I'll send you the link to schedule our interview.

I began using this script when I was 19, hence the X-years-old part of my ask. To be honest, I don't always personalize these emails since Breakthrough Success is a weekday podcast versus a weekly podcast. However, when I see the opportunity to personalize, I am sure to do so. Personalizing your ask will separate you from the crowd.

Get A Calendar App

While podcasting is a great way to build relationships and boost your exposure, there are some challenges with it. Growing your audience, getting sponsors, and asking people to leave reviews are some of the things you need to do.

But the most frustrating thing about podcasting is the back-and-forth emails to schedule interviews and reschedule them when the timing doesn't work. It can drive anyone crazy, especially as you get deeper into podcasting and are in dozens of these back-and-forth email conversations at the same time. Some potential interviews between me and some of my guests almost or completely fell through the cracks because the rapid back-and-forth is hard to keep up with.

One of the best decisions you can make as a podcast host is investing in a calendar app whether it's Acuity, Calendly, or something else. Some of these apps go for a little under $10/mo, and you get to display your available hours. Since using Acuity (my preferred choice although I've seen a lot of people use Calendly too), I have 1-2 back-and-forth conversations every quarter.

Those conversations now only happen when someone isn't available on any of the times I've designated on Acuity or there's a specific timeframe we need to do the interview by. The other 99% of email correspondences are more fluid. I send a link for the potential guest to schedule and that individual picks a time that works for both of us.

Organize Your Calendar To Get The Most Done
Giving your guests a link to your calendar makes it easier for them to find the right time for both of you. The calendar is supposed to provide a convenient schedule for your guest...and you.

One of the mistakes I see people do is always make themselves available. You can go through someone's calendar and find many hours of availability to be a guest on their podcast or have them on your podcast.

Your podcast is an important way to produce content, learn, and build relationships, but creating new episodes isn't the only responsibility you have for your brand. You may serve clients, create content for your blog, send email broadcasts to your audience, create training courses, write books, and do a bunch of other things.

List everything that you do for your brand in addition to your podcast. Once you have everything written down, then batch each of those activities and determine the times and days of week you'll focus on each of those tasks.

For my podcast, I choose to conduct interviews on 1-2 days of the week depending on my school schedule. During summer, I pick one day of the week to conduct all of the Breakthrough Success interviews. That gives me six other days for the rest of my brand. Each day holds a different meaning for me. Tuesdays are solely content creation days while Thursdays are solely marketing days with the exception of writing more content for an upcoming book.

If you make yourself available every day, it is more difficult to commit certain times and days to specific tasks you must perform to grow your brand. Once you identify everything you must do, it's easier to determine when to schedule interviews for your podcast without it cutting into everything else you're doing. Once you strike this balance, you can continue on the road to growing your podcast, producing more content, and growing in the other key metrics of your brand and life.

Chapter 3

The Interview Flow

Now that we've covered how to find and get guests on your podcast, let's cover the interview itself. Each interview needs to flow like a conversation from start to finish. The best podcasts don't feel like rapid fire Q&As. The conversations sometimes meander in different directions because the *organic conversation* meanders in different directions.

It's not uncommon for me to write a bunch of questions and cover few of them. Sometimes I only cover half of the questions I wrote because the conversation takes a different direction. In other cases, I ask all of the questions I wrote down but in a different order. At other times, I come up with follow-up questions based on a guest's answer.

You won't be crisp on Episode 1. I surely wasn't, and every honest podcast host can testify to the same thing. However, you can take action steps now so you are more crisp for your next episode.

Preparation Precedes Success

If you look in any dictionary, you'll see that preparation precedes success. The same holds true for each episode, and on a deeper level, anything you do that is worth pursuing. Your preparation style will change as you do more episodes and get a better feel for your format. However, I want to offer you some pointers to help you get started.

#1: Write The Guest's Bio: The first step to prepare for each episode is to write the guest's bio. You can easily find most people's bios on their blogs' About Me pages and use what's there. As you write the bio, replace any references to the guest's name as "Today's guest." When you introduce your guest, you don't want to mention the guest's name until the very end to build suspense. Yes, people can see who's the guest based on each episode's title, but you'll build a level of excitement by building up to the moment you introduce the guest by name.

#2: Come Up With A Topic: Once you write the guest's bio, it's easier to come up with a topic since you know a lot about the guest. Once you come up with the topic, it is then easier to write questions.

#3: Come Up With Just Enough Questions: You don't want to write too many questions. It's better to let the conversation flow and ask follow-up questions to fill in the gaps. If you write too many questions, it's tempting to ask all of those questions instead of the questions you should really be asking. Let the conversation change direction if it will provide more value to your listeners. You'll get better at asking follow-up questions as you conduct more interviews, but by writing fewer questions, you spend less time preparing for each episode. It also helps to have a set of evergreen questions that you can ask anyone who comes on your podcast (i.e. What is one big challenge you faced on your journey and a powerful lesson you learned during that challenge?).

#4: Read The Bio Out Loud Before The Interview: You don't have to read the bio out loud with the same enthusiasm you'll have when you're recording. However, it helps to read it before the guest calls in. The brief minute rehearsal will help you deliver the intro more effectively during the recording.

#5: Recording The Interview: The Skype Call Recorder and Zoom both get the job done. Whichever option you prefer, test it out with someone else before a guest calls in. This preparation step primarily applies to new podcasters and seasoned podcasters who want to try out a new tool.

Advanced Prep: Knowing Your Content Brand's Portfolio
An advanced preparation tactic is to create a list of all of your content assets to create your own content portfolio (I'm a Finance Major and investor...hence the fancy words in this sentence). Categorize your top blog posts, videos, and past episodes. This will seem tedious but give you ample opportunities to promote your existing content during episodes.

The show notes are a very underrated factor towards having a successful podcast. Some people read the show notes to determine if they should listen to an episode. Some of your listeners will visit an episode's show notes because you referenced several key resources.

The more resources you can mention during each episode, the better your show notes will be. We'll talk more about writing show notes later on, but to come up with these resources, you need to firmly establish the top assets in your content brand's portfolio.

If you are interviewing a guest about making money with webinars, you can look through your content portfolio to find some of your blog posts, videos, and past episodes that can relate to some aspect of making money with webinars. When appropriate, you can mention some of your pieces of content.

Let's say in that interview, we talk about people who are on the fence about starting a webinar. After the guest gives his advice on this topic, I can recommend my blog post "5 Reasons To Host Your Own Webinars" as additional reading. Furthermore, I can tell listeners that the link to that blog post will be in the show notes.

You don't want to mention a new resource at the end of each question. You want each of your resources to organically flow in each conversation. When you recommend one of your pieces of content, make that recommendation as if you were talking with your friend. Would you make a new recommendation every two minutes, or would you only make a few recommendations that were relevant and truly stuck?

You can only make recommendations if you have your content brand's portfolio organized and in front of you while you prepare for each episode. But with a content portfolio, you can make recommendations that lead people into a rabbit hole through your content.

The beauty of a great show notes page is that it may include several links to your existing content. Let's say you mention five of your pieces of content during the episode and link to all of them in the show notes. Let's say you get to mention 2 blog posts, 2 podcast episodes, and 1 video to reach our total of five pieces of content.

Within each of your two blog posts, hyperlink to at least three of your additional, relevant blog posts. Top bloggers frequently link to their older blog posts in their newer blog posts. Some of these bloggers will even edit their older blog posts just to include some links to their newer blog posts.

When you promote a video, never promote it as a standalone. Promote it with other videos. A while ago, I created a video entitled How To Get More Blog Traffic From Siri. If I mention that video in an episode, I would never promote that video's individual link. Instead, I would promote my Blogging Playlist. When people click on the link, they see the entire playlist, but it just so happens that the How To Get More Blog Traffic From Siri video is the selected video.

Viewers get to watch the same video, but some of those people will now view more of my videos since the Blogging Playlist is readily accessible. As an added bonus, you can mention some of your previous videos or blog posts within the video you mention during the episode.

If you repeat this process for more of your podcast episodes, then anytime you promote a previous episode, you are lengthening the rabbit hole. Some of your listeners may then go to your show notes page and find themselves consuming your content for hours without end.

You can best create this effect by mentioning blog posts, videos, and past episodes in each future episode. That way, regardless of how your listeners prefer to consume your content, there's plenty of it waiting for them. You can only get this effect with your podcast if you are very intentional with organizing the assets within your content portfolio and producing more assets that fill in some of the existing gaps.

Bulk Up Your Content Portfolio By Mentioning Content Before You Create That Content
Let's return to the hypothetical situation where your guest is talking about how to make money with webinars. Let's now say that the guest brings up some ways to attract more attendees into your webinar. Furthermore, let's say that you haven't produced a single piece of content about attracting more attendees to a webinar or aren't sure.

During the episode, mention that you'll include a blog post, video, or podcast episode in the show notes with some additional tips on attracting attendees to your webinar. As soon as the conversation concludes, look through your content portfolio to see if you have a blog post, video, or podcast episode (depending on which piece of content you specified during the episode) about attracting more attendees to your webinar.

If you created and published that piece of content, then you're in luck. Just put that link in the show notes. If you check your content portfolio and don't have a piece of content about attracting attendees to your webinar, then it's time to start creating.

Depending on the backlog, I record Breakthrough Success episodes 2-3 months before they get published. This gives me a 2-3 month window to create any content I promised my listeners that I haven't created yet. Similarly to how people use down payments as leverage in real estate investments, you can leverage time to your advantage.

You don't need the final piece of content ready at the time of the conversation. As long as that piece of content is published when it counts—when that episode is published—you're on time and providing that promised resource to your listeners. This tactic will also help you get out of any creative block you encounter since the deadline will be looming over you until you get it done.

As a side note, that's why I decided to do a preorder promotion for Podcast Domination. The preorder gave me a limited window to write this book. While I could have ignored the preorder date and not published this book, it would have meant forfeiting any sales and growth in addition to losing the opportunity of offering my books for preorder for an entire year.

Let Each Question Flow Into The Next
One of the points I mentioned earlier is that a podcast interview isn't just a Q&A. It's a conversation. Like any conversation, the content of your interviews should properly flow from one point to the next. Asking about one thing and then following up with an unrelated question doesn't give the impression of a conversation taking place.

When you write the questions, anticipate follow-up questions. Let's say you ask a guest how to find prospects. Your guest will share some ways to find prospects. At this stage of implementation, you have found some prospects. Of course, you can't do that during the interview, but you know where you are. At this stage, you have found prospects. Now, ask yourself this question: Why is finding prospects important?

It's not the type of question you'd ask a guest on your show. Chances are you already thought of a few reasons prospects are important. Here are some:

1. Prospects can become clients
2. Prospects can refer more clients your way
3. Prospects may consume more of our content.

Chances are there's no surprises with that list. You probably didn't learn anything new by reading that list. However, you now remember a few reasons why prospecting is important, and each of those reasons can be shaped into a question. Let's revisit those reasons prospecting is important and turn them into questions.

1. Prospects can become clients: How can we get prospects to become clients?
2. Prospects can refer more clients your way: How do you ask a prospect if they know anyone interested in my product or service?
3. Prospects may consume more of our content: How can we get prospects to engage with more of our content after the call?

The key to come up with great follow-up questions is to understand the importance of the answer given. What's the value in the answer and the next steps in the process. After you find prospects, the next step is to turn them into clients. After getting someone to visit your blog, the next step is to get them to join your email list. You can continue this next step thinking as you come up with more follow-up questions.

Prepping The Intros For Each Episode

Each episode has its preparation requirements. If you don't prepare before interviewing a guest, you won't know which questions to ask or what to discuss during the interview. Last second preparation will prevent you from getting a great experience from the interview because you'll feel rushed.

You want to prepare well in advance for any episode. I'll focus on preparation for this part of the book as if you're interviewing someone in each of your episodes since a solo show is more straightforward. For a solo show, you just write down the idea and list some things you'd like to cover. When you feel ready, you can start recording. There's no rush, but you do need to establish a routine.

For an interview, there's a set time and date that you need to be ready by. As you interview more people on your podcast, you'll have to do more prep work. I interview anywhere from 5-10 guests for my podcast each week since I host a weekday show. I strongly recommend interviewing as many people as possible because you learn so much from the interview...but the amount you learn depends on your prep work.

The introduction is the most important part of each episode. Intros set the tone for how the rest of the episode will go. If you read a great intro, your guest will be pumped. Bad intros make the episode feel more like a drag. Listeners can tell whether the guest is pumped or not, and the intro plays a key role in determining how pumped the guest is.

And yet almost everyone messes this up. I actually messed this up for the first 94 episodes of my podcast. During those 94 episodes, some people complimented me on the quality of my intro, but it's nothing compared to what I do now.

Most people start by introducing the guest and reading up a bio. As you listen to more podcasts, you'll see how common it is. This is how I used to read my intros:

> Hello and welcome. I am your host, Marc Guberti, and this is the podcast for marketers and small business owners who are looking for the breakthrough for their businesses. I am very excited about this episode. For Episode X of the Breakthrough Success Podcast, we are going to talk about [TOPIC] with our guest [NAME OF GUEST].
>
> 1 PARAGRAPH BIO ABOUT GUEST

You can still spotlight your guest in the intro and make it shine, but it's nothing compared to the new format. I can't move any further in the book without mentioning Michael O'Neal who gave me this intro and forever changed my podcasting career. It's a different type of intro where you introduce the topic and then talk about the guest. Instead of mentioning the guest's name at the beginning, you mention the guest's name at the very end of the intro.

This intro style is similar to what Jimmy Kimmel and Jimmy Fallon use. While these two comedians are better known for the laughter they generate from their audiences, they have to deliver an epic intro to get everyone interested in the rest of the show.

With these two comedians and Michael's advice in mind, here is the new intro I created:

> Hello and welcome. I am your host Marc Guberti, and this is the podcast for entrepreneurs who are looking for the breakthrough for their businesses.
>
> 1 PARAGRAPH ABOUT TOPIC
>
> 1 PARAGRAPH ABOUT GUEST REFERRING TO THE GUEST AS "TODAY'S GUEST" (Note: I never mention the name of the guest until I welcome him/her onto the show).
>
> Today's guest for Episode 115 of the Breakthrough Success is none other than [NAME OF GUEST].
>
> [NAME OF GUEST], it is such as a pleasure to have you on the show.

These new intros get listeners hooked to the episode earlier by building up the topic and guest before welcoming the guest on the show. It's different from what listeners have heard on most podcasts because most podcast hosts conduct their intros similar to my former style. My intro was further enhanced by my incredible podcasting coach Justin Schenck. We changed the beginning where I greet the listeners. Here are the old and new intros.

Previous Intro:

> Hello and welcome. I am your host Marc Guberti, and this is the podcast for entrepreneurs who are looking for the breakthrough for their businesses.

New Intro:

> Welcome…...to Breakthrough Success….I am your host Marc Guberti, the content marketing expert…bringing you 5 NEW episodes a week where I and top level guests teach you how to take your business to the next level and achieve your breakthrough!

To find the meat and bones for the intro, I'll go to someone's About Me Page to read their bio and learn their story. As you interview more people on your show, more people will contact you with potential guests on the show. I've already booked dozens of guests based on other people's recommendations, and the best part is that these guests almost always come with a 1-sheet pitch. That makes it much easier for me or any podcast host to do the prep work.

In a 1-sheet pitch, you get the following:

- The guest's bio
- Website(s)
- Potential topics (3-5)
- Potential questions (3-5)
- A few other things as well

With the 1-sheet, I don't have to conduct any research. All of the research is thoughtfully laid out on one sheet of paper. All I have to do is take what's there and modify it when prepping for my show.

Prepping The Questions

When you write the intro, you'll almost always come up with the topic for that episode. You can't write the intro without knowing what topic you'll focus on. Once you write the intro (and therefore know the topic), the next step is to prep the questions.

You should have a few questions that you ask everyone. These answers should be at the very end of each episode. I tend to ask guests these questions:

- Can you provide the backstory on [insert what the guest is doing or working on]?
- What holds most people back from unlocking their potential?
- What's one big challenge you faced and a powerful lesson you learned during that challenge?
- What are three great books we should read?
- What's one question you believe we need to ask ourselves more often?

I always start off by asking for some backstory while I ask the other questions at the end of the episode. These aren't the only questions I ask during an interview. I'll write down a few questions based on the episode's topic.

The amount of questions you write depends on the length of your interview. My interviews last 30-45 minutes, so I need to ask at least 11 questions to reach the 30-45 minute sweet spot. However, I never write 11 questions, and writing 11 questions would be a mistake. I only come up with three new questions for each show, giving me a total of eight.

You may be wondering how I fill the gap so each episode is still 30-45 minutes long. Intentionally asking fewer questions forces me to listen more to my guests. If you write too many questions, you'll feel obligated to ask every question in the order they are presented. I did this for over a year, and I wish I heard about this advice earlier.

Each episode is like a conversation. I thought I was doing fine by asking my questions in the order I wrote them, but when I tested only having eight questions instead of 11 questions, I realized how wrong I was.

When you have fewer questions than you need, you must pay more attention to what your guest says. If you have all of the questions you need, it's tempting to listen enough to determine how you'll make the transition to the next question. Once you discover how to make the transition, you're so focused on making the transition that you don't listen to the guest as much as you should.

I only have a basic idea of what I need to ask the guest. Three questions guide me in the overall topic, but depending on where the conversation goes, I sometimes never ask any of those questions. Don't ask your questions. Ask the questions that flow from the conversation. If your guest mentions something important that you didn't cover in your questions, don't ask your next question. Ask about that thing you originally didn't cover.

Pre-Interview And Post-Interview

In any call with a guest, there are three parts. The middle part, the recorded interview, is the part you publish on your podcast. However, there are two other parts of each call—the pre-interview and the post-interview.

In the pre-interview (usually 2-3 minutes), you and your guest get to know each other a little better, establish ground rules for your episode, and ask each other questions. The pre-interview ends with you beginning the recording for the episode.

When the episode conclude and recording stops, you have entered the post-interview. The two staples of a post-interview are thanking the guest for being on the show and inviting them to share the episode (emphasize that it is up to them. I usually say something like "I'll send you the link to the episode when it goes live. Share or don't share it. It's entirely up to you"). Most people end up sharing the episode anyway, but you want to leverage permission marketing. Don't try to push the guest into sharing the episode because those types of relationships don't end very well (or end right there).

After you address those two staples, a few interesting things can happen. Here are some of the things that have happened to me during post-interviews.

Not all of them happen on the same post-interview but some happen during the same call:

1. I make new connections
2. I provide the guest with new connections
3. The guest schedules a free strategy session
4. I hire the guest to be my coach (the interview ends up being the application)
5. One of us makes an ask. I've asked different things based on where I was on my journey and my guests have asked me of different things.

The length of a post-interview varies for each guest. I've had 10 minute post-interview conversations that got more exciting as each minute passed by. I've also had 30 second post-interview conversations because I had another guest waiting for me since I record most of my episodes on the same 1-2 days of the week (during the summer, I pick one day of the week, and during the school year, I pick two days of the week to conduct podcast interviews).

The post-interview tends to flow better if you know a lot about the guest. Knowing more about the guest leads to a more dynamic interview, and you'll have a better idea of how to develop and strengthen a mutual relationship. The level of opportunities that can come your way through enough post-interviews can change your life. I recommend doing your best to carve out at least five minutes in-between interviews for the post-interview. It's that important, and I usually end interviews within 40 minutes or earlier so I have more time for the post-interview conversation.

Promoting Your Cornerstone Content During The Interview
During the interview, you have the opportunity to promote products, services, and additional content. However, if you promote too many things, your listeners will feel like you're selling to them instead of providing value.

One thing to think about as you prepare for an interview is how you can organically insert promotions throughout your interview. We will talk more about organically promoting offers, but you should have a plan for promoting your cornerstone content.

Your cornerstone content is your best content not just in value but also in popularity. Giving your most popular content a boost will result in a boost from Google, YouTube, and/or iTunes depending on what kind of content you produce and promote.

Once you identify several pieces of your content that are the most popular and that you're the most proud of, it's time to group them together. I group my blog posts and podcast episodes based on the topic: content marketing, productivity, social media marketing, specific social networks, and a few other categories. The moment I get significantly more active with creating videos, I'll start grouping videos as well.

The idea is to bounce your listeners around multiple formats of your content. Some of your podcast listeners will never watch the video on your YouTube channel, but now they know you have a YouTube channel. During the few times these listeners go on YouTube, they'll think of you. When I realized that some listeners prefer podcasts, I decided to launch the Breakthrough Business Mentor Podcast. It's a daily short-form podcast that I can cross promote on Breakthrough Success and see better results since it's something else people can listen to as they wait for the next Breakthrough Success episode.

With that said, some of your listeners will consume more of your content regardless of whether you have a second podcast, a blog, a YouTube channel, or all of those. When you have people consuming more of your content, the relationship between you and your listeners begins to grow. If you promote a piece of your content in every podcast episode you create, you can create a powerful loop that turns listeners into super fans.

When I promote a blog post on Breakthrough Success, I will edit that blog post before it goes live and link out to some of my other blog posts and podcast episodes. Sometimes I even embed one of my YouTube videos or playlists in that blog post if it's appropriate. Make it as easy as possible for people to surf your content, and you will achieve massive results quicker than you imagined.

Organizing Round Table Conversations

If you get guests for your podcast, you may want to organize some round table conversations on your show. Get three people you know to commit to the same time and ask them questions. Some of the questions you ask can be specified towards one person in the round table episode while other questions can be for all of the guests in that episode.

Round table episodes are a little more difficult to organize, but when those episodes go live, you'll have more people committed to promoting that episode. If you can organize a weekly round table discussion, you can set your podcast up for massive growth.

You can reach out to past guests and invite them to be a part of a themed round table conversation. Theming your round table conversations in advance helps with contacting the right potential guests who have the right skill set for the conversation. You don't want to gather a bunch of random people for the round table conversation and discover they have nothing in common.

As you reach out to potential guests, it's important to reach out slowly for each themed round table conversation. You can reach out for multiple round table conversations at the same time. The danger lies in contacting too many guests for the same round table conversation.

The ideal round table conversation consists of 2-4 guests. Any more than that, and you run the risk of some guests not getting their proper say in the round table conversation. If each round table conversation lasts 30 minutes, and you have 10 guests on the round table, then each guest averages three minutes. Some will go beyond the three minute allotment and that will restrict some guests to under two minutes of audible time on the episode.

A smaller group allows each guest on the episode to provide more insights which will ultimately result in a better episode.

Organizing Round Up Episodes
While the round table format supports 2-4 guests on an episode, it's still possible to publish a valuable episode with dozens of

guests. The secret to producing episodes with that many guests is to turn them into round up episodes.

Instead of managing a dialogue between guests on a round table, you ask people to answer one question and send their recorded response to you. By inviting 10-30 people to share one quick tip based on a specific theme, you'll have a lengthy and valuable podcast episode in no time.

The round up episode presents an interesting opportunity where you don't have to do much of the content creation on your end to come out with a full length podcast episode. For a round up, all you have to do is record yourself introducing the round up and the wrap up. You can share follow-up insights after some of the guests' tips and add other audio clips in between each guests' responses, but all you need to provide at the least is the intro and the conclusion to the episode.

Similarly to a round table conversation, it's best to have a theme for the round up episode before you start reaching out to potential guests. That way, potential guests better know how to serve your listeners. When the episode gets published, you'll have even more people eager to promote the episode versus a round table conversation.

Both round ups and round table conversations take some time to set-up, but they can have a powerful effect on your podcast's growth and your listeners' experiences as they go through your podcast's episodes.

Chapter 4

Post-Production Adjustments

Very few podcast episodes gets published as their raw files. Once the post-interview is over, the post-production phase begins. The post-production is designed to polish your episode and promote some of your offers.

The Intro And Outro

The intro and outro are audio clips that you add to the beginning and end of each episode respectively. Both of these audio clips form the bookends of each episode. In your intro, briefly talk about the show and present one of your offers. At the beginning of each episode, in between me talking about Breakthrough Success and the episode topic, I include an intro clip promoting something I'm working on.

Whether it's my book Content Marketing Secrets, a free strategy session, the Content Marketing Success Summit, or something else, I'm always promoting something I'm working on at the be-ginning of each episode. The outro is a longer clip that goes into greater detail about one of those offers since it's at the very end of the episode. If people reach the end of your episode, they'll proba-bly listen to you talk about your offer for 30 seconds.

While many podcasters leverage the outro to promote one of their offers, few podcasters leverage their intro. The intro is one of the best places to put an offer because everyone who listens to the episode will know about your offer. If you only mention your offer at the end of each episode, you need someone to listen to the EN-TIRE episode. While it's possible, why talk about your offer 30-45 minutes into an episode when you can mention it 1 minute into the episode?

And you can do that without turning people off (although I would never run a sponsor ad at the very beginning of any episode. It's a bad first impression for new listeners and is different from briefly talking about one of your offers first).

Some listeners will pay attention during the intro when you men-tion your offer. Some of your listeners will believe the offer is a valuable can't miss since it's coming from you, a person they have learned to know, like, and trust.

Write The Script And Get It Right Once
The great thing about post-production is that you can improve the way you sound in the episode and add audio clips to any point of the episode. Instead of mentioning the intro and outro when recording episodes, I record the intros and outros in advance.

Recording the intros and outros in advance gives me time to write scripts and literally read the scripts right off my computer screen. I don't ad lib any of the intros or outros I use for Breakthrough Success episodes. The intros and outros are meant to be concise, and filling any part of the intro and outro with uhhs and umms doesn't create that concise experience your listeners expect.

Often, the intro and outro are utilized to promote something you're working on or have just completed. As a bonus, you can incorporate music within your intros and outros. While you don't want to incorporate too much music (listeners won't pay as much attention to what you're saying in the intro. They'll be listening more to the music), you can use music to lead into your intros and outros.

Before we get into an example of some intro and outro scripts, notice how I'm implying that you'll utilize multiple intros and outros for your episodes. Some of your listeners will binge through your episodes.

If you keep using the same intros and outros, your listeners will get conditioned to them and skip to the next part of the episode similarly how everyone clicks on YouTube's "Skip Ad" button the moment they can. Fine, not everyone clicks on that button right away, but you get the idea.

That's why I have a few intros and outros in place. Each episode gets one intro and one outro, but I like to mix them up so the same intro and outro don't always play at the start and end of each episode.

Determining What To Promote In Your Intros And Outros
You can promote sponsors in your intros and outros, and we'll cover that later in the book. However, I want to go a little deeper

and expand your thinking for what you can promote within these segments of each episode.

What you promote in your intros and outros boils down to your KPI and nothing else. KPI stands for key performance indicator, and it's the one thing that matters more than anything else. The fewer KPIs you have, the better. The only three KPIs that matter for me are revenue, client acquisition and email list growth.

Sales and clients matter because your business can't survive without them. Email list growth matters because that asset can fuel the growth of all of your other assets (i.e. podcast, book sales, blog traffic, etc.).

What are your KPIs that you use to determine if you're succeeding or falling behind? Those are the KPIs that you need to focus on with your podcast's intro and outro.

One intro I use on Breakthrough Success invites listeners to schedule a free 20 minute strategy call with me. Here's what that script looks like:

"What's up achiever? Before we get started with today's episode, I like to offer you a free 20 minute strategy call. In that strategy call, we'll talk about what you can do to grow your business and how we can work together to achieve your breakthrough. To schedule your free 20 minute strategy call, head over to marcguberti.com/strategy which will be in the show notes. Now, let's get right back into today's episode."

That's not the same intro I use in every episode. I use that intro in at least one episode each week. The other intros I use are also KPI-focused. If something doesn't align with one of my KPIs, I don't consider it. Furthermore, I look at different offers I can mention in the intro and outro with the mindset, "Does Offer A help with my KPIs more than Offer B?"

If I promote two landing pages, and Landing Page A converts better than Landing Page B, I'm not going to promote Landing Page B much longer. As soon as I write up another intro, I am going to test that intro against Landing Page B. The intro that converts the best is the intro I will use. The same applies for outros.

While it's hard to track direct conversions with a podcasting format, I look at conversion rates all across the board. I take the total visitors the page has and divide that by the total occurrences of the desired action (i.e. new subscriber, a scheduled 20 minute call, etc.)

However, this is where KPIs matter again. I mentioned three KPIs, but my most important KPI is revenue. You need sales to keep the doors open and continue making your payrolls. Here's a scenario that demonstrates the power of focusing on the right KPIs.

Landing Page C has a 40% conversion rate. If 100 people visit that landing page, 40 of those people subscribe.

Landing Page D has a 20% conversion rate. If 100 people visit that landing page, 20 of those people subscribe.

Guess which one I'm promoting. Landing Page C, right? Not so fast.

Let's now say that Landing Page C's email sequence has a 5% conversion rate. If 40 people go through that email sequence, 2 people will buy the product in that funnel.

Let's also say that Landing Page D's email sequence has a 20% conversion rate. If 20 people go through that email sequence, 4 people will buy the product in that funnel.

Do you see how getting 100 visitors for Landing Page C only results in 2 sales while getting 100 visitors for Landing Page D results in twice as many sales? Even though I get fewer people on my email list, Landing Page D looks like the winner since I make more sales by promoting Landing Page D.

But I care about revenue, not sales. Let's say the product in Landing Page D is priced at $100 while the product in Landing Page C is priced at $500.

For Landing Page C, 100 visitors results in two sales. 2 x 500 = $1,000
For Landing Page D, 100 visitors results in four sales. 4 x 100 = $400

Focusing on the wrong KPI can send you the wrong signals. Let's say that you create the holy grail of landing pages that gets a 100% conversion rate. Every person who visits that landing page joins your email list. If that landing page gets 100 visitors, you've got

100 subscribers. That's the landing page you have to promote, right?

But what if none of those people ever buy your products, click your links, or opens one of your emails? Do you still want to promote that landing page?

I can easily turn this into a massive rabbit hole. Maybe your email sequence isn't good enough, and you need to modify that. The landing page is just fine. Maybe for Landing Page D, you can easily charge $500 for your product and make $2,000 when 4 people buy it.

Know your KPIs and how to optimize them before you promote anything ever again. You could optimize for a 100% conversion rate for your landing page but not make a single penny for your business. Landing page optimization is just one piece of the system.

The Script Rubric

Phew! I almost went too deep into that rabbit hole, but I felt it was important to include that in Podcast Domination even though I kind of went on a tangent. Let's get back on track and talk about the intro script I shared earlier. We are going to take a deeper look at that intro script so you can discover how to craft your scripts.

What's up achiever? — I welcome the listener. Notice that I don't say listeners or achievers. I keep it singular. Make each listener feel like you're talking to them as an individual instead of an entire audience where they're just one person in a sea of many.

Before we get started with today's episode, I like to offer you a free 20 minute strategy call. — I mention the episode will start soon and what I want to offer. Notice how I include the word free. That's one of the best words you can use in your copy.

In that strategy call, we'll talk about what you can do to grow your business and how we can work together to achieve your breakthrough. — The benefits are laid out and it's about the listener, not me. Some people focus on sharing the product features without honing in on how the listener would benefit.

To schedule your free 20 minute strategy call, head over to marcguberti.com/strategy which will be in the show notes. — Call-to-action with an easy to remember link and telling listeners that the link will be in the show notes. That way, they can take action after the episode (some of your listeners will listen to your podcast while driving. Taking action on the spot isn't possible for these folks).

Now, let's get right back into today's episode. — Transition into the episode

Your intros and outros should each be 30-60 seconds long. While your intros and outros can be shorter than 30 seconds if necessary, you don't want them to last over a minute. Starting each episode with a 2 minute delay into the actually content will turn listeners away from your podcast. While there aren't as many podcasts as blogs and YouTube channels, there are still enough options available for your listeners if they don't like the experience you're providing.

Intros and outros are important for you to grow and monetize your podcast, but don't make them too long. You can use the same intro script for your outro with a few changes which I've bolded in this comparison.

Intro Script:
"What's up achiever? Before we get started with today's episode, I like to offer you a free 20 minute strategy call. In that strategy call, we'll talk about what you can do to grow your business and how we can work together to achieve your breakthrough. To schedule your free 20 minute strategy call, head over to <u>marcguberti.com/strategy</u> which will be in the show notes. **Now, let's get right back into today's episode."**

"Want to grow your business? I like to offer you a free 20 minute strategy call. In that strategy call, we'll talk about what you can do to grow your business and how we can work together to achieve your breakthrough. To schedule your free 20 minute strategy call, head over to <u>marcguberti.com/strategy</u> which will be in the show notes. **Keep dreaming and keep achieving. Your breakthrough is coming."**

Instead of greeting your listeners a second time, you ask a question that leads into your offer. Further more, you end with a slogan in your outro instead of leading people into the episode like you do with the intro.

Those rubric scripts are valuable not just because of what they contain, but also because of what they don't contain. Notice how I don't thank my listeners for listening to the episode.

I don't say, "Thank you for listening to today's episode," in the outro…and I don't plan on it. With that said, I am grateful for everyone who listens to an episode, but there's one reason I never mention this in the outro.

"Thank You" signifies the end of the episode. Your listeners will pick up on it and use "Thank You" as the indicator to skip to the next episode or do something else. They won't listen to the last 30-60 seconds of your outro. Remember, these listeners made it to the end of one of your episodes. They are committed listeners and very likely to engage with what you share in the outro.

"Thank You" takes away a ton of engagement and visibility from what you promote in the outro. That's why I don't thank people at any point in my content unless it is at the very end (not close to the end but literally at the end. Anytime I say thank you in any piece of content, I thank them and end with my slogan).

Inserting Thoughts During Episodes
When you finish recording an episode, the episode itself is not finished. So far, we've focused on inserting sponsor snippets and polishing the existing episode. In addition to these post-production adjustments, you can also insert snippets of additional content into your episodes.

When I interviewed John Lee Dumas, I only had 15 minutes to ask him questions. With that little time, I didn't start by asking for JLD's backstory. His backstory is on EOFire's site, and I briefly recapped that backstory in an audio file I included before the audio file containing my interview with JLD. I also inserted other audio files throughout the interview where I expanded on some of JLD's answers and talked about how his insights have impacted me.

In a similar fashion, you can insert some of your thoughts in between your guests' answers. One thing most hosts don't do is share more of their own knowledge with their listeners. Asking great questions and getting even better answers isn't enough. You need to bring your own value to the table to increase the overall value of each episode and your podcast as a whole.

Some hosts accomplish this with mini episodes each week. My friend and podcast coach Justin Schenck records short 5 minute episodes each week on the Growth Now Movement Podcast in addition to weekly interviews. People don't just listen to Justin's podcast to hear from the guests. They also want to hear more from Justin, and he adds additional value every week with his solo appearance episodes.

You can insert various thoughts throughout your episodes or create standalone episodes like Justin does. Either way, you need to constantly think about how you can provide more value than what you're already providing. You can publish an extra episode each week with another guest or just you sharing some insights in a few minutes. You can ask more questions or reference more resources in each of your episodes. Write a list of all of the ways you can provide more value to your listeners, and commit to checking off everything on that list within each episode.

Inserting your thoughts in between episodes is more important for round-up and round table episodes. During a round table, you can share some of your thoughts about each guests' answers to your questions. When organizing a round table, make sure you highlight different things that all of your guests say. You don't want to play favorites on the round table.

For a round-up, you've got a bunch of people submitting an audio clip containing their responses to your question. Some of those responses will sound very similar and cover the same insights. You can space these audio clips at different points in the episode, but you can add a new twist on one of those insights by sharing some of your additional insights. You can also comment on how a guest's answer resonates with you.

Let's say you ask 20 people for their favorite productivity hack. If one of those 20 guests shares a productivity hack that you also use, tell your listeners that you use that productivity hack too. You can share how you use that productivity hack and how it has impacted your productivity. Your listeners want to hear more of you, and inserting your thoughts throughout each episode will provide a more valuable experience for your listeners.

Writing The Show Notes

Every podcast needs show notes. Depending on the format of your episodes, some of those show notes will be long while others will be short. Regardless of the length of your show notes, they give your listeners an extra place to go for information. Some of your listeners will listen to your podcast on their commutes. Even your most loyal listeners probably won't pull to the side of the road to write down a link you mentioned in an episode.

This is where the show notes come in play. Your listeners will have a better experience because they don't feel the pressure to remember every small detail. Not only that, but if you place the show notes on your blog, your listeners might stick around and read some of your other content.

Make Your Show Notes A Cut Above The Rest
Most of the show notes you come across will contain nothing more than a guest intro, a few key points, and some links. If a listener writes down all of the links and a bunch of notes, there's no strong incentive to visit the show notes page. I followed the traditional format for over 200 Breakthrough Success episodes.

Then I listened to the Side Hustle Nation Podcast hosted by Nick Loper. I've listened to the podcast before, but after Podcast Movement 2018, I listened to his podcast with a new mindset: How can I make my podcast better. He incorporated a bunch of things I was completely missing out on, but the most glaring difference turned out to be the show notes.

Nick didn't just provide an intro to the guest. Nick also shared how they met at a conference (if applicable), his thoughts, and most importantly, uses the show notes to tell a story about the guest. That story is designed to cover the beginning of the guest's journey and how the guest got to where they are now.

You should write the show notes to each episode as if people were deciding based on the show notes if they should listen to your episode or not. Nick also includes Pinterest optimized pictures in his show notes to encourage people to share his content. Pinterest is one of the most underrated social networks for gaining visibility for your podcast. Long, bright pictures with words on them (headlines, quotes, etc.) tend to win.

Some people will read your show notes before they listen to the episode. While you don't want to give too much away in the show notes, you also don't want to make the show notes so brief that they don't encourage people to listen to your episode. The title of each episode carries more weight than the show notes, but they carry considerable weight when people read them before listening to the episode, especially when the person viewing the show notes hasn't listened to your podcast yet.

Taking Notes During An Interview
If you interview people for your podcast, it's important for you to take notes during the interview. Taking notes will help you create better show notes for your listeners. Granted, I delegate most of the show note responsibilities to my assistant (i.e. quotes, listing book recommendations, etc.), but I write up the introduction for each episode's show notes.

During the interview, I'll write down some tidbits that strongly resonate with me. If the tidbit is very long, I'll look at the Skype Call Recorder and type the time of the tidbit. For instance, if one of my guests is saying something very insightful at the 7:27 mark, I write down 7:27 on my notepad.

When taking notes during an interview, it's critical that you write the notes on a notepad instead of typing them out. While typing isn't very loud, it is loud enough to cut into the audio, especially since the typing happens right where you are recording the episode. You listeners don't want to hear you typing in the background. Writing down your notes on a notepad allows you to avoid creating the background typing noise.

If you host your own podcast or are a co-host, most of the note taking will take place before an episode so you're well prepared. At the end of each episode recording, jot down some quick notes of things you want to mention in the show notes. Yes, you could replay the episode and then write the notes. However, writing down notes while you remember everything will save you time. Save time like that with hundreds of episodes, and that extra time starts to add up in a big way.

Editing Your Episodes
I can't provide too much on this topic because I haven't edited an episode on Breakthrough Success. This is one of the activities that I decided to delegate from the beginning so I could focus on other parts of my podcast.

If you want to do basic editing where you just splice out mistakes, any option will work whether it's iMovie, Screenflow, or even QuickTime. If you want a more advanced free tool, Audacity is a free, reliable option while Adobe Audition is a more advanced tool that requires a small investment.

I am intentionally being vague with what it takes to edit episodes because this is not my speciality. It's better to double down on your strengths than it is to spend time on weaknesses that you can easily delegate.

Delegating These Tasks
Out of all of the stages in podcasting, the post-production is the one hurdle that some people don't jump over. This is the big hurdle that I couldn't jump over in my prior attempts to starting a pod-

cast. I had recorded episodes ready to go, but I never got around to doing the post-production work.

If you find yourself having difficulty doing any part of the post-production work, delegate that work to someone else. I never edited any of the Breakthrough Success episodes because I knew handing myself that responsibility boosted my chances of being inconsistent and possibly giving up on the show.

Some people love editing their episodes, but that wasn't me. There are some things you'll enjoy about podcasting and some things you won't enjoy about it. Delegate the things you don't enjoy so you can focus on doing what you do best.

I still recommend jotting down some notes before, during, and after each episode because it will help you remember more of the insights from the episode. This is especially true if you interview guests on your show. Some of my biggest breakthroughs and lessons learned are a direct result of what past guests have taught me.

The best place to go for finding talented people internationally is onlinejobs.ph. The platform is filled with highly talented and dedicated job candidates. With that said, it's important to still do your due diligence. Interview each job candidate and ask a set of questions. Determine how each candidate can perform the task and who would be great to work with. I always look for a solid work ethic and a kind heart.

You can look for different values and skills in an ideal candidate, but make sure you know what those values and skills are before you reach out to people on onlinejobs.ph.

Chapter 5

Podcast Marketing

You now know the amount of work it takes to produce a new episode for your podcast. Maintaining and growing your podcast is an investment, and to the get most bang for your buck, you need a solid marketing plan for each episode you publish.

However, the marketing doesn't start on the day your episode comes out. The marketing starts earlier than that.

Laying The Foundation
Before we dive into some of the advanced techniques, we need to master the basics. Luckily, there are only two basic element that make a strong foundation. The first basic element is consistently publishing new episodes on your podcast.

If you publish an episode each Wednesday, continue doing that and let your audience know they can expect a new episode next Wednesday. That's as simple as saying, "Welcome to the [name of your podcast] where we provide [benefits from your show and pain points you solve] every Wednesday..." or something similar at the start of each episode. Consistency is key, but you have to let your listeners know about your consistency for it to work.

There's another element to building a strong foundation. I'd say that it's an element at least 90% of podcasters overlook. It took me almost two years to actually discover this basic element even existed. Most people never think about it. There's two parts to this critical element:

1. Determining your avatar
2. Interacting with your audience

When you create a new episode, you should create that episode for someone instead of your listeners. Create an imaginary person in your mind and create podcast episodes for that person. If you create this imaginary person correctly, you'll end up creating episodes that your listeners will enjoy. These are some of the questions to ponder as you create this imaginary person which we'll now refer to as an avatar:

1. How old is this person?
2. Is this person employed or unemployed?
3. Does this person have a family or is he/she single?
4. What is this person's gender?
5. What are some of this person's pain points and aspirations?

Asking and answering these types of questions will give you a better idea of who your listeners are. While this is a great approach to creating better episodes and doing better marketing, we've got one flaw in the previous statement.

This will only give you a "better idea" of who your listeners are. It's a start, but it's not a complete picture. You get the complete picture by interacting with your audience. You may have interacted with your audience through social media, replying to emails, and responding to comments, but there are two key ways to interact in a powerful way.

The Power Question

"What's the biggest struggle you're currently facing with/regarding X?"

Ask that question, and you'll get a bunch of answers. Ask the question to more people in your tribe, and you'll find more overlap. You may discover that most of the people in your tribe want advice on using Facebook ads. You may also discover that content creation isn't a big challenge for most of the people in your audience.

Create episodes that address your listeners' biggest challenges. Your job as a content creator is to create content that is relevant for your targeted listener (also known as your avatar). Once you create episodes for your listeners instead of solely for the sake of producing something new, you'll be on the right track to success.

Get On The Phone With Your Listeners

One of the best investments of your time towards growing your podcast is getting in more 1-on-1 phone conversations with your listeners. Not only can you get a deeper understanding of your listeners' biggest struggles, but you also build a culture of super fans.

I have been involved in many product launches, and my favorite launches involved conversations with the person I was promoting.

Two of my favorite training courses are Copywriting Academy and Self-Publishing School, and that's not by accident.

Not only are those courses incredible, but I've had 1-on-1 time with both Ray and Chandler. They were both guests on my podcasts at times corresponding to their product launches. In addition to those podcast appearances, I got a private 30 minute call with Ray and met Chandler in-person at Podcast Movement.

In the prior examples, there was a decent time investment. Each of my episodes are 30 minutes long, so Ray and I talked with each other for a little over an hour. Chandler and I talked during our Breakthrough Success episode, and we briefly talked in person for about two minutes. However, you don't need 30 minutes to make a big impact on your listeners. Just the sole fact that you picked up the phone or decided to give your listeners a call will show that you care.

I once had a brief 3-5 minute phone call with someone, and I've been a super fan ever since. I was involved in two of this individual's launches and received copies of two of his books. I knew I'd already be meeting him at one of the stops for his book tour, but that brief 3-5 minute phone call was just with me. He thanked me for supporting his launch and asked a few questions about some of the projects I was working on.

He honestly didn't have to call me. I would have shared his book with my audience regardless. It's a book I had already read and re-read leading up to the launch. But that's why Daymond John is known as the People's Shark. Knowing he made the time in his schedule to have a quick 3-5 minute phone call with me made me feel a sense of gratitude. I was acknowledged for my efforts to help spread the word by the man himself.

It's easy to get on the phone for 3-5 minutes and talk with one of your listeners. It's even easier to not do it. Daymond John is careful with how he uses the hours in his day. If the famed Shark Tank investor believes making phone calls to his audience is important, then you know it's something you need to do more often for your podcast—especially when you are just starting out.

Notice that I mentioned Daymond John, Chandler Bolt, and Ray Edwards in this book. I am a super fan, so talking about those three comes natural to me. You may have seen that in the way I recounted everything that I have a deep appreciation for all three of them. I am a super fan of a few other entrepreneurs and brands, but this rift isn't leading to a list of everyone I'm a super fan of. Rather, this is how other people will promote you when they are your super fans.

It's the book mentions, conversations where your name pops up, and other types of recommendations that increase your reach. Most of those recommendations will come from your super fans. If you want more super fans, start talking with more of the people within your audience.

Get On More Podcasts
Consistency, determining your avatar, and getting on the phone to turn listeners into super fans forms the foundation for a successful podcast. Now we go deeper into tactics you can start using to boost your visibility.

One of the best ways you can grow your podcast is by being a guest on more podcasts. I've asked many podcast hosts the "How do you grow your podcast?" question or something similar to that. Almost all of them pointed back to getting on more podcasts. Why is this strategy so powerful?

For a podcast, your audience doesn't just consist of people interested in your niche. It consists of listeners who are interested in your niche. You can write guest posts which help with marketing, but some blog post readers may not care too much for listening to podcasts. Even though I host my own podcast, I know that I consume way more blog posts than podcast episodes. Although I don't advise it, you can technically host your own podcast without listening to a podcast.

Instead of focusing your podcast marketing efforts on guest blogging, appearing on other shows is the path to victory. Since I host a business podcast, I aim to get interviewed on business based podcasts. That way, I get in front of an audience of people who are interested in growing their businesses.

But even better…they are podcast listeners. I don't have to tell them how to listen to a podcast (more on that very soon) or download an episode. People listening to a podcast know how to find other podcasts to listen to. I just mention the name of my show during the interview, and some of those listeners will choose to check out my podcast and subscribe. Get on more podcasts, and you'll continue attracting more listeners to your podcast.

The Podcast App Isn't Enough

Not everyone knows what a podcast is. Some people think they don't have a Podcast App installed on their device. Most smartphones such as the iPhone come with a Podcast App automatically installed. It's one of those apps you get along with the Phone and Camera apps and all of the other ones you can't delete.

Some people don't know where to access podcast episodes. One of my friends mentioned YouTube as the place to find podcast episodes. I then showed everyone the Podcast App available to them and mentioned Stitcher and Spotify as other options.

Because of my efforts, a few more people know they have a Podcast App on their smartphone. However, there are many other people who believe YouTube is the place to find podcast episodes. Others don't know and aren't interested...yet.

If you limit yourself to the Podcast App, you miss out on a large segment of your potential audience. The solution is to repurpose your content. We already covered show notes which are great for incorporating your podcast episodes into your blog feed. However, you also need to repurpose on YouTube. Not only do some people believe podcasts are on YouTube, but YouTube is something that everyone understands. My dad doesn't have a Facebook (you read that right), but he watches YouTube videos.

Podcasting is a dynamic way to produce content that millions of people know about. But there are also millions of people who don't know what a podcast is. Publishing your episodes on You-Tube will help you reach a larger listener base.

I probably know what you're thinking. You may like the idea but argue it's time consuming and can be costly. I avoided YouTube for a while for those two reasons. We've got so much to do as podcasters already. Uploading each episode to YouTube takes a lot of time.

Until Repurpose.io stepped into the picture. After you provide Repurpose.io with your podcast feed URL, it will take all future episodes and automatically publish them as YouTube and/or Facebook videos depending on what you prefer. You can also take a Facebook Live, automatically turn it into a podcast, and have that automatically turned into a YouTube and/or Facebook video as well.

It's a truly brilliant low-cost tool that will save you hours of time every week while putting your episodes in front of more people. You can learn more about the tool at marcguberti.com/repurpose and get your first month free. Yes, that is an affiliate link, but I am a strong believer in this resource, and I've shown that with the monthly payments I make to Repurpose.io

Break Down Your Episodes
If you interview guests on your podcasts, some of the episodes can stretch past 30 minutes with some of those episodes even stretching past an hour. Not all of your listeners have the time in their schedules to listen to episodes over 20 minutes. Those listeners may only have time to listen to your podcast during their commutes.

To cater to these listeners and provide a valuable experience for the rest of your listeners, you can take a snippet out of one of your previous episodes and turn it into a standalone episode. Lewis Howes does this the best on his School of Greatness Podcast. Every Friday, he publishes a snippet of a previous episode. He refers to each snippet as 5 Minute Friday episodes which are usually five minutes long.

Not only does this provide a valuable experience for your listeners and help with commuters, but you can also use this approach to bring back older episodes. At the end of each snippet, you can say something like, "Want to listen to the rest of this episode? You can either scroll to Episode #X or go to [link] to listen to the entire episode."

If you create multiple podcasts (more on that later), you can use this tactic to cross promote your podcasts.

Outreach Leads To Growth
At it's core, there are two principles to growing your audience. The first principle is to tap into your existing audience, develop a culture of super fans, and they'll spread the word about what you do. The second principle is to reach beyond your audience and build new relationships.

If you host a podcast with guests, outreach will be a requirement. You can't get guests on your show unless you reach out to people. This is why I strongly recommend having guests on your show. It helps with knowledge acquisition and marketing. On the day the episode goes live, email the guest with the link to the episode.

Many of the guests will share their episode with their social media audiences which means more listeners for your show.

At one time, I published five interview based episodes each week on Breakthrough Success. I've dialed it down a little bit because consistently listening to five episodes each week is a strong commitment for any listener with other podcasts available. This publishing frequency helped me grow my listener base big time because at least five people shared their episode with their audiences each week. The compounding effect allowed me to quickly get thousands of downloads each month.

While emailing each of your guests when their episode comes out is a great marketing tactic for your podcast, it's something you won't always be able to do. Sometimes, you may send that email 1-2 days late. I found myself responding late to several guests, and with five episodes each week, the late emails stockpiled.

All of that went away when I came across the Spark App. Almost by accident, I came across the inbox app because Apple's Mail app had a bug at the time (now fixed). I continue using Spark because of how easy it is to organize your inbox. Best of all, you can schedule certain emails to get sent at certain times.

As I wrote about Spark, I realized that it was past 9:30 am eastern, the time I'm supposed to email my guest about their episode getting published on Breakthrough Success. I forgot to write and send that email, but Spark had me covered. I usually write 30 emails at one time and schedule them all in advance. The show notes link to every episode is marcguberti.com/e# (replace # with the number of the episode) and the iTunes link is marcguberti.com/itunes. The nature of these links makes it easy for me to schedule months of emails to guests in advance. That way, I don't have to remember every day, and I still get the boost when guests share their episode with their audiences.

Social Media Marketing For Your Podcast

No good marketing book would be complete without mentioning social media. The platforms allow you to grow your audience and connect with it in a meaningful way. Leveraging social media can be the difference between a popular podcast and a podcast that only gets a few downloads for each episode. Social media isn't the only way to grow a podcast, but each platform can yield life changing results.

When you publish a new episode, let your entire social media community know about it. Tweet about the episode at least four different times on the day it comes out. Create pictures for Instagram (400x400) and Pinterest (600x900) for each podcast episode. I use Canva to create a framework for each picture and have my assistant create pictures based on the title and guest for each episode.

Depending on your podcast's topic, LinkedIn may be a great place for you to promote each episode. LinkedIn is filled with business savvy individuals which makes it a great opportunity for business based podcasts. You can find potential guests for your podcast on LinkedIn by using their search feature and filtering it so only people show up in the search results.

I intentionally left Facebook as the last social network I'll cover here. You can share each new episode on your personal account and your Facebook Page. That will help drive more exposure. But if you want game changing results from Facebook, you need to start a group for your podcast.

That group will build a sense of community between you and your listeners. However, not only will your relationship with your listeners be strengthened, but your listeners also get to interact with each other. Listeners can share their takeaways from each episode and get likes and comments from other listeners. Facebook Groups turn fans into super fans, and if you combine that with occasionally calling some of the most active people in the group, you'll foster a highly engaged community.

Using hashtags helps with the marketing, but at its core, social media marketing is telling your audience about each of your new episodes and building a community. Start funneling your other social media followers to your email list AND your Facebook Group. Growing your audience is important, but growing a community is even more important. Set up your social media strategy so new followers become a deeper part of your community instead of just another person in your audience who only knows you but no one else who listens to your show.

Have A Plan For Promoting Your Newest Episodes
We covered a lot of ground in the Podcast Marketing portion of this book. There are many additional ways to market your podcast episodes, but these tactics and strategies tend to be the most effective.

Now you have to create a plan for how you'll promote each new episode. List the different tactics you'll utilize and try to delegate as many of them as possible. Each time a new episode gets published on Breakthrough Success, here's what happens with that episode.

1. It gets tweeted out to my audience
2. An Instagram picture gets published
3. It gets pinned to my Pinterest board
4. The episode gets mentioned in a LinkedIn update
5. That episode gets shared with some of the people on my email list
6. The guest receives an email that their episode has been published
7. Some episodes get posted to the Facebook Group (I avoid posting links into the group as often as I can)
8. The episode is automatically published to my YouTube channel

Someday, that list will get bigger. It may consist of 10 or even 20 different things I'm doing to promote each new podcast episode. However, most of those tasks will also be delegated. Of this list of eight tactics, I'm only scheduling emails and posting to the Facebook Group on the day of a new episode release. All of the social media activity is delegated (I write the copy in advance), and I write the emails several weeks in advance and schedule them using the Spark Inbox app.

Chapter 6

Monetizing Your Podcast

Now that you know how to grow your podcast, we're going to dive into the exciting part. Making money from your show. While most people are quick to think about landing sponsorships, there are plenty of additional ways to monetize your podcast. We'll begin by talking about sponsorships and then expand into some of the other ways you can monetize your show as well.

Getting Sponsorships

Out of all the monetization tactics, getting sponsorships for your podcast is perhaps the most known but also the most confusing. How do you approach sponsors? How do you even find the right one?

Before you think about approaching a sponsor, you have to demonstrate you have a large audience. The larger your audience, the more likely you are to land a sponsor. Even if you don't think you have a big audience yet, do as good of a job as possible at positioning yourself that way.

For instance, if you don't have many podcast listeners, but you have a massive social media audience, you can leverage that when getting sponsors for your podcast. You can say that in addition to getting a sponsor ad on your show, you'll also promote them to your social media audience. The more you give, the more likely a potential sponsor is to say yes.

You can start reaching out to sponsors who would be a great fit, but one of the best tactics you can use is reaching out to brands that already sponsor other podcasts in your niche. These brands know the potential of a podcast sponsorship and understand how they work. After you reach out to a few other brands to get a feel for sponsorship outreach, tell brands currently sponsoring other podcasts that your podcast is the next great destination for them.

Once you find a good fit, the delivery is essential. Most people write an email, list their audience sizes across different platforms, and list some of their rates. If you want to stand out, don't do what most people do. Instead of typing a long email, create a short slide deck containing the info potential sponsors need to make their decisions. Not only will a slide deck allow you to more easily convey sponsorship info, but it will also make you look more professional. Perception is reality, and a well-designed sponsorship slide deck indicates you take your craft seriously.

When you create the slide deck, include the following on separate slides:
- Your podcast's name and logo
- Your podcast consumer's avatar (age, when they listen, interests, etc.)
- Metrics (total downloads, average downloads per episode, number of new episodes each week and year)—also decide if you will charge per episode, for all of episodes in a given week if

you create more than 1 episode each week, a set quantity of episodes, or some other method

- Sponsorship and Partner Rates (mention what you'll do and the price points)
- Team (if you have assistants and a bunch of people on your team, this creates a strong perception that you take your podcast seriously)

The slide deck will significantly boost the number of sponsors you land for your show. However, understand that you may get plenty of rejections in the beginning. Just keep going at it and some sponsors will eventually say yes.

Affiliate Sponsorships

Let's say you can't find a sponsor to pay you right away. That doesn't mean your podcast will never make money. There are plenty of additional ways to monetize your podcast, and one of them is affiliate sponsorships. While traditional podcast sponsors may turn you away, an affiliate program almost never will.

One popular affiliate program podcast hosts like to promote is Audible. Someone listening to your podcast may also be interested in listening to audiobooks. If you send a lead Audible's way, you earn $15. If three of your listeners buy Audible, you make $45. You can also look for other affiliate opportunities with high conversion rates and hundreds of dollars in commission for each sale you make.

I have my own affiliate program which focuses on digital marketing related products, and if you are interested in making a 50% commission from everything you sell, please reach out to me through my email marc@marcguberti.com. Beyond my affiliate program, you can find many great products to promote using ClickBank, LinkShare, and ShareASale among others. If you use those three affiliate programs, chances are you'll find hundreds of products in your niche that you can readily promote and start earning commissions.

Promote Your Own Landing Page

While promoting other brands and other people's offers can help you monetize your podcast, you should always promote at least one of your landing pages during each episode. Through a landing page, you can grow your email list (a critical asset for any business) and generate revenue from the autoresponder.

Promoting your own landing page doesn't give the same impression as an ad for another person or sponsor. Some of your listeners want to hear what you're up to, and promoting your landing page is a way to tell your listeners what you've been working on lately.

The great thing about promoting your own landing page is that you have complete control over the backend. If Product A isn't converting very well, you can better optimize it or replace it with Product B. You can add a 1-click order bump to your product to boost your revenue per customer. You can add an upsell later on or change the upsell based on conversion rates and revenue potential.

While there are plenty of ways to generate revenue with a podcast, incorporating your own landing pages should be a top priority. Your listeners will come to appreciate the value you're providing on the show. They'll also appreciate recommendations you make as an affiliate, but they want to know what you're offering too. If you tell your listeners about an offer you're providing, your listeners will be more likely to go to the link that you mention during the episode.

Use Optimize Press To Create The Landing Pages
Creating landing pages and connecting them to email sequences is one of the most powerful ways to generate revenue for your business. While there are plenty of options for creating your own landing pages, only two resources truly matter...LeadPages and Optimize Press. LeadPages is a great resource for creating landing pages, but Optimize Press is the best option because this WordPress plugin allows you to create landing pages, membership sites, homepages, and just about everything else you need to have a successful website for your podcast. Optimize Press is perhaps the most important plugin you can possibly install on your WordPress site.

Organically Insert Promotions Into The Conversation
The best way to promote an offer on your podcast is to organically mention it in the conversation. Many podcast hosts leverage the first 30 seconds of the episode to promote an offer. While this seems like a smart strategy since more people will hear the offer, few people listen all the way to the end of an episode. The only danger with promoting an offer at the very beginning of your episode is that new listeners may feel turned off if your episodes start off with offers. That's why you need to incorporate certain promotions throughout your episode. Not all of these promotions can be planned, but some can be.

Here's how a planned organic promotion plays out on Breakthrough Success. I always ask Breakthrough Success guests for great book recommendations. After they provide their recommendations, I mention that those book recommendations will be in the show notes. I will also mention a book I've recently published or am currently working on. The moment I realized I'd be writing Podcast Domination, I started promoting the book before I finished writing it. I drove many initial pre-order sales that helped me pay for some of the production expenses for this book.

The moment I come up with another book idea, I'm promoting it on Breakthrough Success before it's ready. Sometimes I also link to a landing page promoting one of my free books to give my email list a boost. I change up the book promotion depending on what my goals are for that moment.

You can also organically insert promotions into the conversation by interviewing the product creator or someone who has a success story with using a certain product. Earlier in the book, I mentioned Chandler Bolt and Ray Edwards. Both of them were guests on Breakthrough Success, but the timing of the interviews was intentionally planned. Both interviews came out during their training course launches. During these interviews, I promoted my affiliate link and received a commission for each sale I made through the podcast. You can ask any product creator if they'd like to be on your show and be willing to provide you an affiliate link you can use to make a commission for each sale.

Charge Guests To Be On Your Show
When my coach first recommended to charge guests to be on my show, I felt a cringe. At this time, I had interviewed over 200 people and not charged a cent for it. I wasn't afraid to charge $1997

for a training course, but charging guests felt like something I shouldn't do.

Then my coach and I talked about my audience. At the time, I had over 500K social media followers, 10K email subscribers, and 88K Udemy students (who I could email). He mentioned people would pay a fair amount of money to get in front of that type of audience, and he argued I could charge a good amount of money for someone to be a Breakthrough Success guest.

However, he only recommended I charge for guests who reach out to me. If I reached out to a guest, I couldn't charge them. If I determine a guest can't pay my fee, I invite them to buy one or more of my books instead. This was one of the strategies I used to drive initial sales to Podcast Domination. I asked my guests to buy the book during the post-conversation, and anyone who reached out had to buy the book to be a guest on Breakthrough Success.

Your guests are getting in front of a massive audience by being on your podcast (even if it's just 100 people), and you can ask for a favor in return. Not every guest bought the book but most of them did. Just ask and see what happens. Most guests are happy to help you in some way for the exposure you're giving them.

Turn Your Podcast Episodes Into Products
When I launched the Breakthrough Business Mentor Podcast, my goal was to provide daily bite-sized insights that would help listeners grow their online businesses. As I planned out the episodes, I realized I was hitting on certain themes that could be expanded upon. The list of episode ideas began to look like multiple book outlines meshed together.

When I saw the episode ideas as an unorganized book outline, I realized I had struck gold. I could repurpose the Breakthrough Business Mentor episodes into books and strategically release episodes on similar topics. When I come up with a new book idea and do the outline, I turn as many of those main points into Breakthrough Business Mentor episodes as I can. I'll add some additional insights into the book but most of the content for these particular books will be based off the Breakthrough Business Mentor Podcast.

Turning podcast episodes into books is also an economically sound move compared to actually writing them. The average person types just 40 words per minute, and while I can get on a hot streak and hit 80 words per minute while coming up with ideas, it pales in comparison to how many words we can speak in a given minute. It turns out the average person speaks about 100-130 words per minute according to Word Counter. That rate reigns superior to my 80 words per minute which I don't always maintain. Even with an outline, I still have to come up with ideas as I'm typing, so I don't always type 80 words each minute. However, ideas flow out more easily as you're talking which explains how the average person can speak 100-130 words per minute.

I would argue that I speak over 130 words per minute and can consistently hit 150 words per minute because of the hundreds of episodes and thousands of videos I've produced over the years. If I can hit 150 words per minute speaking and 80 words per minute typing (assuming I can consistently type at that pace without taking breaks or having to think a little bit), I can complete a book almost twice as fast by speaking it.

The best part is that the book comes out over time. It isn't something I have to sit down and think about for a few hours. I write a book outlines and turn parts of those book outlines into episodes. It's the only effective way I know of to write multiple books at the same time. You can get any audio transcribed with Rev.com at a rate of $1 per minute. While these costs may add up as you produce more episodes, you can anticipate this ahead of time and gradually transcribe episodes or know that you have to generate more revenue from your podcast to make the investment to transcribe the episodes.

While Rev.com is the common choice for audio transcription, Sonix (Sonix.ai) is increasingly presenting itself as the better choice for audio transcription. At a $15/mo retainer, you can get your episodes transcribed at a rate of $5 per hour which far surpasses Rev.com's $1 per min rate which comes to $60 per hour The best part is that Sonix will provide you a free 30 minute trial which allows you to see the quality of their audio transcriptions before you commit to a plan.

Sonix will provide you with the transcribed audio in a few minutes instead of several days and provide you with an SEO friendly approach. I always mention rev.com because it's usually the go-to for audio transcription, but if you plan on transcribing your podcast episodes, Sonix is the smarter choice.

Some people turn their podcasts into successful products that become significant streams of revenue. In 2015, a soon-to-be podcaster wrote an essay about his five favorite New England myths.

While he originally intended to give the essay as a free PDF, he recalled that the word count got out of control.

Aaron Mahnke then decided to turn that content into a podcast. *Lore* was born. Since it's 2015 launch, the widely acclaimed podcast has been spun off into several books, merchandise, and even an Amazon Prime TV Show. Aaron focused on providing valuable content to his listeners. He didn't go into *Lore* with a plan to turn the episodes into books and a TV show. His focus on providing valuable content and promoting that content eventually resulted in a massive community of *Lore* lovers.

While *Lore* is an example of a storytelling podcast, there's plenty of room for growth with information based podcasts such as business podcasts. Gregg Clunis launched his Tiny Leaps Big Changes podcast in 2016. Two years later, his podcast now has over 3 million downloads, and it's now becoming a book called *Tiny Leaps, Big Changes: Everyday Strategies to Accomplish More, Crush Your Goals, and Create the Life You Want*

The possibilities for turning your content into products and merchandise are endless. However, a common theme is a strong focus on providing valuable episodes. The books, merchandise, and TV shows came later. Producing massive value while expecting little in return came first.

Leveraging Your Podcast To Attract Clients
Client attraction is one of the top ways to make money with your podcast. With the right service and pitch, you can land $997+/mo clients with your podcast.

Get 9 of those types of clients from your podcast, and you're at a nifty 6-figure income. Get 21 of those clients and you're making over $250K every year.

The math adds up, and the best part is that client attraction isn't the only way you can make money with your podcast. Some people listening to your show won't want to become your clients right away.

You need to strengthen the relationship with them through your episodes and get them to put some skin in the game. "Putting skin in the game" is marketing talk for turning a listener into a customer, even if it means a $1 purchase.

It's very easy to create something and charge $1 for it. In most cases however, you're better off pricing that product at $7 or at $5/mo to boost your profitability.

The product I promote on Breakthrough Success depends on the timing. I promoted Podcast Domination in every Breakthrough Success episode a few months before its release. The book was $0.99 during preorder, and that small skin in the game increases the likelihood of future purchases.

Remember, at $997/mo, you only need 9 clients to make 6-figures. You just need 6 clients if you raise your services to $1497/mo.

How To Charge Those Kinds Of Prices
For some people, charging $97 for a consultation session is difficult. Technically, it's easy. Just change the order page or PayPal button to reflect the new price. However, some people don't be-

lieve their consultation session is worth $97. These people are underpricing themselves.

Other people command $1997 price points just to spend an hour with them. There are services that cost five figures each month, and some people have no problem writing a $1 million check for a Lamborghini.

$997/mo is the example I've used, but if you can (note: yes, you can) charge higher than $997/mo, then you will need fewer clients to hit your income goals.

Ask yourself what it would take to double your price without doubling the time you spend on each activity. You don't go from $97 to $197 by going from a 30 minute consultation session to a 1 hour consultation session. How can you make that same earnings jump without the extra 30 minutes?

The two answers to this question are to demonstrate your expertise and showcase your credibility. It's no wonder the highest priced products and services are flooded with testimonials.

Want to get high profile testimonials? It's not as difficult as you think. Interview high profile guests on your podcast. Build relationships with them. Tell them about your product or service and offer it for free (for an ongoing service like scheduling social media content, offer one free month).

Then you'll start getting testimonials from key players in your niche. Some of those same people may become clients or buy a bunch of your products. Even if none of those key players become long-term clients, those testimonials will provide you with strong social proof as more people come across your products and services.

Notice how the podcast helps with a key element in converting people into clients? If you do it right, you can also use the podcast to demonstrate your expertise as well. You can release a solo episode every week, share insights in between a guest's answers, and do a bunch of things to demonstrate your expertise during each episode.

So How Do We Actually Get Clients

The previous portions of the book about attracting clients have been the set-up.

Most prospects turn into clients through free strategy sessions. Almost everyone in the business leads people into a free strategy session to convert prospects into clients. Anytime I've hired a coach, I made that decision based on a free strategy session.

If you want clients, then you will need an Acuity account. Acuity makes it easy for you to create a calendar that only shows the times when you are available. That way, it's easier for prospects to pick times that work for you instead of engaging in a back-and-forth conversation to find the ideal time.

If you even have to engage in that kind of back-and-forth conversation, you will lose clients.

Acuity is the best option available, but it comes with a universal problem all calendar apps come with. The long link problem.

Remember, you're goal is to recruit clients with your podcast. If we were talking about blog posts, you could easily include a hyperlink to your schedule page and move on.

But with a podcast, that option doesn't exist. You have to verbally say what the link is. I ran into this problem when promoting my book Podcast Domination. On a blog, I can just include that hyperlink in there.

On a podcast, I have to figure out how to tell people to visit this link:

https://www.amazon.com/gp/product/B07FSHGR9N

I'd have to say Amazon dot com slash gp slash product slash B07FSHGR9N during the episode. That's hard to say while keeping the episode natural. It's even harder for a listener to remember.

Especially if that listener is driving like the 23% of Americans who listen to podcasts in the car.

I took that same link and turned it into this:

www.marcguberti.com/pd

Much easier for me to say and even easier for a listener to remember.

Marc Guberti dot com slash P D is much easier for people to remember than the other one.

How do you create links like this? If you have a WordPress powered blog, I recommend the Pretty Links plugin. It's the one I used to create the link above, and I also get to track stats. By creating a custom link for my podcast, I can track how many clicks can be specifically attributed to my podcast.

You can do the same thing with bit.ly links. You can customize the text that appears after the slash. The link http://bit.ly/podcastdomination also gets you to the book's Amazon Page.

The only danger with using bit.ly is that your ideal link might be taken. For instance, bit.ly/pd will send you over to someone's Flickr Profile. Therefore, I can't use that customization to link to my book.

Turn Existing Relationships Into Joint Ventures
Podcast monetization isn't just about what's happening within each episode. Podcast monetization also occurs on an indirect level based on how much you allow the deep relationships you develop to continue growing.

Some of the people you interview on your podcast may become part of a joint venture you organize someday. They may promote your products or buy your books. One of the ways I drove sales to this book was mentioning it to every guest I had on the show during that preorder phase of the book. During the preorder phase of Podcast Domination, I set the price to $0.99 to drive more sales (I do this for most of my preorder book launches). Many of those guests ended up buying the book because they were happy with their experience on my show and $0.99 is a small investment in building a relationship.

You can also create a product or service and invite some of your past guests to participate as affiliates. While there are several factors that go into deciding who I reach out to for Breakthrough Success, one of those factors is to see if the guest could be an affiliate for one of my products. Each episode is relationship building in its finest form. Think about what kind of people you want in your network, and seek them out. You can initiate the relationship by inviting those people to be guests on your podcast.

Use ThriveCart For Affiliate Related Joint Ventures

If you want to leverage your podcast to recruit affiliates, you need to have a solid affiliate program in place. Many of the affiliate programs I've participated in over the years have used Infusion-Soft. While InfusionSoft is a great resource for setting up an affiliate program, it's very expensive. There's a mandatory kickstarter coaching one-off cost of $1,999 in addition to paying hundreds of dollars every month to maintain the affiliate program.

Instead of going with InfusionSoft, I decided to create my first affiliate program with SamCart. Access to your own affiliate program on SamCart costs $197/month which doesn't seem like a lot if you're running a successful affiliate promotion. However, there's an even better option. ThriveCart is that better option with one lifetime payment of $595. That way, you don't have to continue paying hundreds of dollars each month. One $595 lifetime payment for ThriveCart is the equivalent of three monthly payments on SamCart.

Not only is ThriveCart the better economical option, but it's the best affiliate program software I've used. ThriveCart allows you to create slick sales pages with 1-click order bumps, upsells, and downsells. They also make it easy for you to view your affiliates' links, see how each affiliate is doing, and know how well your sales pages are converting.

You might not need be thinking about recruiting affiliates for a joint venture right now, but if you do, I wanted to plant the seed now that ThriveCart is one of the top options available. You can also massively grow your audience and bottom line by organizing your own joint ventures, but that goes beyond the scope of this book. Another incredible opportunity you may want to consider is running multiple podcasts which we will discuss in the next chapter.

Chapter 7

Running Multiple Podcasts

Running multiple shows is not for the faint of heart. It's a big time commitment, but it's becoming the new frontier of podcasting. More podcasting superstars are making announcements about second, third, fourth, and even fifth podcasts that they're launching.

Before we talk about the work associated with running multiple podcasts, let's talk about the different types of podcasts:

#1: Solo Podcast—You go off on rifts connected to a certain topic. Sometimes it's just you coming up with ideas you know your audience will like based on your phone calls and other interaction. At other times, it's you answering questions your listeners submit.

#2: Interview Podcast—This is the most common approach. A host interviews a guest and asks a few questions. I strongly recommend having at least one of these types of podcasts for the knowledge acquisition and outreach.

#3: Podcast With Multiple Hosts—This is exactly what it sounds like. While it may be difficult at times to match up schedules, it's well worth it. You and your fellow co-host promote each episode and shoulder the expenses together. It's good to have multiple podcasts if you follow the co-host method. While this approach can provide a dynamic experience, I've seen some podcasts disappear because the co-hosts wanted to move in different directions. If you have that goodbye episode, it's good to send people over to another podcast you host.

Why Running Multiple Podcasts Is The New Frontier
We learn differently. It's a well-known truth that can be seen in people who prefer to read versus visual learners. Some people prefer reading blog posts while others prefer watching videos. There are also people who prefer listening to podcast episodes to acquire more knowledge. That's the audience segment we focus on with our podcasts (excluding our repurposing efforts which we use to target audiences who learn in the previously mentioned ways).

While there are overarching ways that we learn (reading, watching, and listening), there are subsets for each of those learning methods. This is where running multiple podcasts comes in. Some people listen to new podcast episodes on their 20 minute commute to work. Most Breakthrough Success episodes average 30 minutes. You can't listen to an entire episode on your work commute.

People on that same commute can listen to 5-10 minute episodes from a daily podcast. Some listeners have a lot of time to spare while others don't. Some listeners enjoy listening to music at the beginning of each episode while others want to get right to the insights. Some listeners enjoy the interview format while others think it takes up too much time.

If you want to cater to multiple preferences that your listeners have, you need to host multiple podcasts with different styles. Some should be daily 5-10 minute soundbites of knowledge while others can be deeper 30-45 minute weekly episodes. Both approaches work, but utilizing both approaches allows you to attract listeners who have a preference for a certain podcasting style.

The Ultimate Cross Promotion Strategy

The average listener is listening to 5-6 podcasts. Becoming one of those 5-6 podcasts in itself is an incredible feat, but what if more people listened to more of your podcasts? What if some listeners heard you interview people and do a solo show? Regardless of what niche you are in, you are competing for your audience's attention. Giving your audience a few extra podcast options can make the difference between some visibility and massive growth.

The great thing about having multiple podcasts is that you can lead existing listeners to your new podcasts. I lead Breakthrough Success listeners to the Breakthrough Business Mentor Podcast. There are two key benefits from this type of cross promotion:

1. **Breakthrough Success listeners spend more time with me**. As they're waiting for new episodes to come out on Breakthrough Success, they can listen to the short daily format provided on the Breakthrough Business Mentor Podcast.
2. **More Breakthrough Business Mentor listeners means more discoverability**. Podcast directories see the surge in subscribers and downloads that came because of Breakthrough

86

Success. Now the Breakthrough Business Mentor Podcast starts to attract listeners outside of the Breakthrough Success community.

And here's the icing on the cake. I use the Breakthrough Business Mentor Podcast to promote Breakthrough Success. Listeners not yet in the Breakthrough Success community are quickly invited to become a part of that community as well. Those two benefits I mentioned earlier now apply to Breakthrough Success as well.

What we have is a positive loop in which listeners spend more time listening to my content and boosting the discoverability of both podcasts. Imagine adding a 3rd, 4th, or even 5th podcast to the mix. The more podcasts you have, the more loops and sub-loops you can create.

This is why running multiple podcasts will be the new frontier. Podcasting is a blossoming space filled with massive upside potential and a smaller crowd than blogging and vlogging. However, some listeners prefer an interview style show while others prefer a quick paced daily podcast. Instead of trying to make your podcast something that everyone will enjoy, you create multiple podcasts to cater to different types of listeners.

Batch The Work
I'm not going to pitch all of the benefits without sharing the workload it takes to run multiple podcasts. However, it's not impossible. Just like any other goal, the key to making this work is scheduling time to do the recordings and book guests for your show. The best way to pursue multiple objectives, especially when it comes with podcasting, is to batch the work.

As I write this book, I'm going into my junior year of college. For my fall semester, I have a lot of free time between my morning and evening classes. Therefore, I designated Monday as Breakthrough Success Day. On Wednesdays and on Mondays when Breakthrough Success interviews are cancelled or rescheduled, I record episodes for Breakthrough Business Mentor. Co-hosted podcasts are a little more difficult because your schedule needs to consistently match with your co-host, but you and your co-host can agree on certain day(s) of the week to record episodes.

The way you batch your work depends on how often you come out with new episodes. On Breakthrough Success, I currently release three new episodes each week. With each call getting a 45 minute time slot, my Monday commitment to the show is 3 hours (I add in an extra call to stay ahead of schedule or in case someone needs to reschedule). While Breakthrough Business Mentor is a daily podcast, the brevity of each episode means I can get about 10 episodes completed in under 2 hours. Managing multiple podcasts may seem difficult, but the moment you think about consistently carving out days and times for specific parts of each podcast, it becomes more manageable.

At this point, I strongly recommend delegating some of the activities within your podcast and other parts of your business. Podcasting is important, but you don't want it to overshadow all of your other initiatives. Podcasting is a great opportunity, but starting and running multiple podcasts is an extraordinary opportunity and the new frontier of podcasting.

Conclusion

Podcasting presents an incredible opportunity for you to create content, learn, build relationships, grow your audience, and monetize your brand at the same time.

Just like any venture worth pursuing, there is no quick and easy path for podcasting. It takes a considerable amount of time and effort to achieve success. However, you can achieve success with your podcast faster by focusing on the podcast and not letting distractions enter the picture.

If you've ever heard of someone who achieved a big goal like six figures in a few months, that's because they put in a massive amount of time towards their craft. Look for the extra minutes and hours in your day to commit to launching, growing, and monetizing your podcast.

You can also speed up your path to success by seeking a mentor who can help you along the journey.

After my private call with Ray Edwards, he told me that I had everything I needed to become successful. I wager that, right now, you have everything you need to become a successful podcaster. If you implement the best nuggets in this book, you will most likely become a successful podcaster.

The key word is implement. In this book, you learned strategies that I've tested on Breakthrough Success and that I've seen tested on other podcasts. These strategies work, but to get the strategies to work for you, you have to put in the work.

I believe you have everything you need. All you need to do is take action. Glean through this book again and identify what you'll do first. You may need to launch your podcast first. That's where creating an account on a podcast hosting site like Libsyn and reaching out to potential guests is a great start. You may already be deep into the podcasting game but not monetizing. In that case, look at your intros, outros, and how you promote new episodes.

Only once you take action consistently and frequently over a long period of time will your vision turn into achievement.

Schedule Your Free Strategy Session

If you want to learn how to grow your brand, you can schedule a free strategy session with me by heading over to <u>marcguberti.com/strategy</u>. I hope to hear from you and see how I can help you grow your brand and achieve your breakthrough.

About The Author

Marc Guberti is a digital marketing expert, entrepreneur, and author with over 90,000 online students. He is the host of the Breakthrough Success Podcast where he and his top level guests teach you how to take your business to the next level and achieve your breakthrough. He is a #1 bestseller on Amazon who has written over 20 books and was ranked as one of the Top 50 Amazon authors in the Business & Investing section. He is a social media columnist for the Westchester & Fairfield County Business Journals. Marc coaches business owners on how to grow and monetize their online businesses.

Other Books

Thank you for reading Podcast Domination. If you enjoyed it, I hope you consider leaving a review on Amazon.

If you want to read more books from me, here's a list of some of my books you can find on Amazon.

Content Marketing Secrets: How To Create, Promote, And Optimize Your Content For Growth And Revenue

77 Powerful Methods To Get More Kindle eBook Sales

Write and Grow Rich: Secrets of Successful Authors and Publishers (Exclusive Tips from Publishing Experts)

How To Be Successful On Twitter

Lead The Stampede: How To Become The Leader Of Your Niche

Outsourcing Domination: How To Win At Outsourcing And Get Your Time Back Now

Pinterest Domination: How To Grow The Engaged, Targeted Audience That You Have Always Dreamed Of

How To Write A Book In Under 6 Hours

Made in the USA
San Bernardino,
CA